Roundtrip

poems by

Dawn Angelicca Barcelona

Finishing Line Press
Georgetown, Kentucky

Roundtrip

ACKNOWLEDGMENTS

The following poems were previously published, sometimes in different versions:

"Portrait in Sepia," *Atlanta Review*, 2023
"Woman Lost While Looking for Stars," *Stoneboat Literary Journal*, 2023
"Dear Violet," "Muse," and "Bilateral Stimulation," *Epiphany*, 2023
"Bloomfield, 1997," *Amongst the Weeds*, Kearny Street Workshop & Asian Art
Museum, 2023
"Carabao," *Mortal Mag*, 2022
"Queen of Scars," *In Parentheses*, 2022
"McDonald's" and "Nearly Imperceptible," *The 2River View*, 2022
"Magpie's," *Tilted House*, 2022
"New Jersey," *Red Ogre Review*, 2022
"December," *Trouble Maker Fire Starter*, 2022
"ASIAN GIRL WANTS TO SEE," *sPARKLE & bLINK*, 2021
"Cake," "Re:," "Upon Arrival," and "Guro Station, Line 1," *The Fulbright Korea
Infusion*, 2017
"A Small Gesture," *In Between Hangovers*, 2017

Publisher: Leah Huete de Maines
Editor: Christen Kincaid
Cover Art: Qing Saville
Author Photo: Samantha Marie English
Cover Design: Elizabeth Maines McCleavy

Order online: www.finishinglinepress.com
also available on amazon.com

Author inquiries and mail orders:
Finishing Line Press
PO Box 1626
Georgetown, Kentucky 40324
USA

Contents

Woman Lost While Looking For Stars

You are a child of the universe no less than the trees and the stars;
you have a right to be here.
    —Max Ehrmann, "Desiderata"

Three-thousand miles away from home,
a woman counts the stars in Badwater Basin.

*

My mother warned me not to look up too quickly,
the sun will bite, your neck might snap. She says *don't answer*
the door for anyone and this refrain pours onward,
until my eyes are covered with stars.

*

If this night went missing, along with this woman,
could park rangers resurface both with one helicopter?

*

My mother held my tongue taut
when I was ready to taste the moon.
She asks if I'll come home by midnight,
as if I could go far. *Many fears are born*
of fatigue and loneliness. This is why I go.

*

I lick my thumb and press
the sky with my fingerprint,
thinking of girls who don't answer,
whose mothers leave voicemails.

*

Somewhere in Death Valley,
a woman sits by a window
so she can watch her daughter.

*

When I come home,
I'll tuck away my stars.

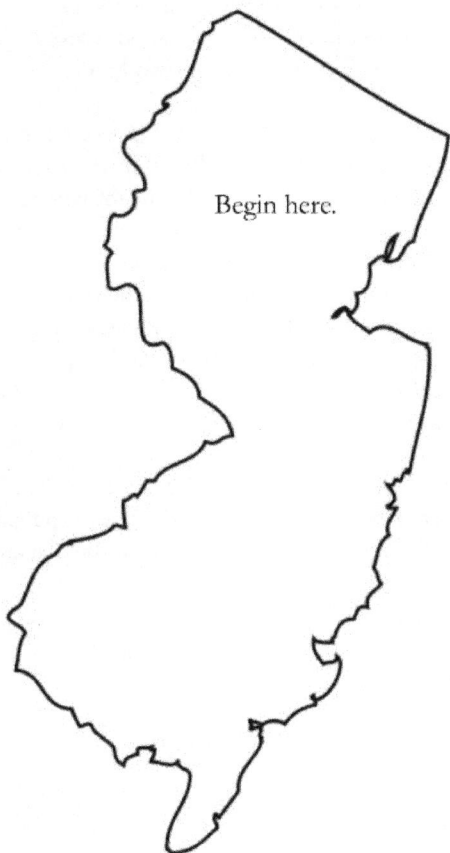

Begin here.

Bloomfield, 1997

I regret nothing about the playground. Like propelling myself face-first
and busting my lip open. The clever way I made myself indispensable
at home with my tears, my laughter, my hunger.

I regret nothing about the blacktop. Like eating rubble then spitting
it out, my blood soiling the white shirt of my uniform. Dribbling
on the tarmac, my classmate runs for our teacher who says *not this again.*
I count the number of times I've done this on two hands.

By November, the principal catches on. She says *if you come to school every day
this month, I'll give you a gift.* Any kid would be bribed by something palpable,
playable, collectible. Did you know what regret meant when you were five?

Every morning, Ms. Giordano pulls me into her office.
At her desk, she slides a thin box in front of me. She opens
it like a book she will read to me. St. Francis of Assisi emerges
in painted stained glass, a man among sheep and goats.
His gift was bloody palms, a sign of the faithful, one who endures
the love of God. The animals lick and lick his wounds dry.

I learn blood is a gift so I return to it again and again on the playground:
a scraped knee, a papercut, a nosebleed, a mouth of teeth pulled
so I wouldn't swallow them as I did with pebbles on the blacktop.

If you were covered in blood,
would someone call your parents?
Or would no one say a word?

I learned to regret my early scars, my endless tears.

One day, any adult will regret asking a kid: *why are you doing this to me?*

McDonald's
a golden shovel after William Carlos Williams

Growing up, it was hard to forgive
my sister when she grew angry, though she took me
away from home when our parents fought. They
thought money and fast food were
ways of saying sorry. Though delicious
as these Happy Meals were, only so
many plastic figurines and nuggets with sweet
and sour sauce could fill up the void love leaves. And
the two of us scarcely hugged each other, except for when it was so
dark outside that we didn't want to lose each other in the cold.

Nearly Imperceptible

When the thread of my being catches the edge of an engine,
I will barely feel the slice.

When the butter knife swipes my bread,
it will hardly leave an imprint.

When this photograph gets wet, it will marble at its corner,
nearly imperceptible.

When the day is done, my computer still hums.
Only then do I feel its heat.

When I grab a towel, the shelf will tremble, then sit still.
Maybe a thing falls - like a sock, scarf, or shirt.

I will find this thing when I move out and bag it up
and realize I never noticed its absence.

My
words
are too
brittle
to make
it back
it back

to you.

Carabao

When polyembryonic siblings fall so far from their tree,
I choose the sweetest mango delicately resting
until the ants or flies or I come to feast.

As I slice through—almost grazing the pit
I nearly scratch the heart of this fruit.
I inspect the fiber and pull threads out with my teeth.

My first mango was sun-dried
emboldened with Manila sunshine and boxed up
like childhood memories in an attic.

My *ate* and I trade toys for the taste of sunshine.
I visit an eternal summer in my sleep
in my dreams I melt into this flesh.

Prayer for My Grandparents, Who Went Too Quickly

I've been to the places where my father began,
where uncle after uncle ended. To say their hearts were broken
isn't sudden enough. They were following their mother's and father's hearts.
Their father went first, then their lonely mother's heart
snapped two weeks later. At 9 years old, my father is an orphan.

Last month, I lit two candles for him on his birthday: a 7 and a 1.
He's outlived his whole family.

I've been to the center of where my mother began, where twins are common
enough to rupture a womb beyond rescue. Upon her eighth child,
my mother's mother ended. My mother had dreams of her mother
slipping out of her urn to ask *do you want to join me?*
And my mother, barely three years into her own body, said yes.
Her living sister scooped her up and said *no, let our mother go.*

Her father was the lifeline that kept the family together.

Every year on Christmas Eve, I sit in the back of a church
and listen to songs about birth, rejoicing, silent, holy nights.
I kneel when I'm supposed to, I take two fingers to my

forehead,

heart,

left shoulder   right shoulder.

My lips almost open, praying:

may their souls and all the souls of the fathers and mothers
(whom I've never met)
say back to me

"amen, amen, I'm resting in peace."

Portrait in Sepia

Cuttlefish shoot smokescreens
then spend hours in hiding.

They hunt with beaks sharp enough
to pierce crabs right to their core.

Their blood—not quite red—
and ink—not quite black—

are the same color to them,
no matter where their w-shaped eyes turn.

Their hypnotic stripes teach
their babies inside how to hide.

Like us, they dream in REM sleep,
jerk awake through their tentacles.

Like me, they are active at night,
stepping through mud and mildew.

And they are also like you,
with three exploding hearts

each beating in a different time zone.

A Small Gesture
for Tatay Tiago

Once, a stranger extended his hand to pull me up La Fortuna in the rain.
I've wondered all these years if this is what your hands would feel like
holding mine when we meet for the first time, unsure if it's okay
to touch me at all, unsure if you could kiss me on the forehead
like you've known me at all. I only remember a single phone call.
Mom held the phone to my ear, *say hi*! I wanted to drop the line.
One day, you would make it to America or I would make it to your home.

I imagine bringing you a plate of food, looking at the callouses that cling
to your palms receiving my gift, me understanding you had a lifetime
of work and it is time to rest, at least for a meal. Finally, I've arrived.

What did your hands do when you weren't eating? I've missed out
on a lifetime of you. I'm sorry I couldn't bring you to what I only knew
and couldn't say enough about with the limits of my seven-year-old
tongue. I always wished I could have said some more. You've been resting
now for twenty years. When I saw your casket, you jumped at me
in your grasshopper body. You followed me into the house you built.

At 18, my tongue was stupid and slow in Costa Rica, my first time
away from mom and dad. This rich coast hardly brings me closer
to where you're from, but it lent an old man's hand to me.
I wondered if his smile was the kind you would have given to me.

I held on tightly and the old man pulled me up like a sack of rice.
Later at the hotel, I imagined the contours of your aged face.

Now I cling to your voice, the words raspy and few,
and my words, stuttering, "I can't wait to meet you too."

ASIAN GIRL WANTS TO SEE

I am short / like the dirty fingers of your hand / I am infantilized / I am fetishized / I am bold like a brush stroke / I am ornamental like a holiday / I am the seasoning to your longing / *langka* / *laaing* / *bangus* / *bagoong* / *sinigang* / *sisig* / *kamayan* / You say / "you come from conquistadors" / the product of rape / the product of imperialism / the product of pity / The ships were sailing in from all directions / to mail our women as brides to be / I was born and bred in this country / You say / "you don't have an accent" / which one you were expecting? / My parents pushed me away / with their absence / The Balikbayan box sits in our living room / I smashed my face on the playground / so I could wait for them at home / My scarred lip needed balm / so my dad mailed it / without coming home / I asked for a toy / on a long-distance call / my dad asked / "what kind of toy?" / I thought he should know by now / When he came back to visit / I looked for my surprise / he pulled out a doll / a baby with a bottle / so pale and blond / why didn't it look like me? / Before I visited his home country / I thought brown skin was beautiful / but suddenly it wasn't / When my mom got a raise / we went to a warehouse / a liquidation sale / Mom said / "get whatever you want" / so we ran through the aisles / me, my sister / and our nanny / (who wasn't supposed to be in this country) / I only knew limits before that day / I remember the taste of the minty chocolate sticks / the beaded necklaces / princess tiaras / pink bubblegum tape / I felt lucky / carrying two trash bags to our car / stuff that was new / unopened / finally ours / When we all lived like a family again / we spent late hours in Atlantic City / I walked the casinos of Caesars and Trump Taj Mahal / heard the jackpot jingling / followed the ball chasing after the roulette wheel / said hi to the fishnet tights of the cocktail girls / my dad felt lucky enough / to lose what my mom made / I saw old ladies in wheelchairs / smoking in the non-smoking section / they were also losing / our skin was not the same / I wanted to change my last name / get rid of our oppressors / I wanted to whiten my skin / lighten my hair / blend in with the crowd / I wanted to find my mom / lost in the quarters sinking deep into slot machines / I wanted to find my dad / and see if we were winning / I wanted to be seen / and when I wasn't / I learned to be alone / alone / alone / when I was alone / and lonely / you'd be surprised by what I could see / now my eyes are wider than you'll ever remember / there are thousands of us gathering / in Atlanta / LA / New York / San Jose / in this country / we know home / we know ourselves / My dad is from Manila / My mom is from Cebu / I am an American

What are you?

Could you tell me
about your last visit?

Cake

We grilled our own meat at Restaurant 108
and drank beers and soju, sitting Korean-style.
We spent too much time teaching our own language
to learn the language of this new country.
We leaned on each other to pick from the few
words sown inside our mouths.
We were just kids wondering how to eat. 어떻게[1] ?

We planted a new alphabet to help us sprout through the soil
of Sejong, a province new to us and new to the country.
With soft-spoken syllables, our courage boils up: 맞아요[2] ?

Back at home, we said "fork" and "spoon" or "please" and "thank you"
now we only point and say "여기요, 이거 더 주세요[3] "
our tongues burn, digging for more words when we see a kitchen.

We set the cake down next to our grill.
Here we sing 생일 축하합니다[4] instead of happy birthday.
The song tastes like an expiration date
another birthday I wish I could be home for, hoping after a year
it will still be waiting for me in the fridge.

1 *Ottoke,* How?
2 *Majayo,* Is it right?
3 *Yogiyo, igeo deo juseyo.* Over here, more of this, please.
4 *Saengilchukha hamnida,* Happy birthday!

Editor-in-Chief

"reiterate too owl:" a phrase still sitting in my email drafts after seven years revisited today to make sense of what I was really trying to do   maybe take notes while I led a staff meeting the editors the submission managers social media manager designer website developer photographer all on Google Hangouts   there was some pre-work that most all finished   they were supposed to read pieces   scrubbed of [IDENTIFYING INFORMATION] and rate them on style content clarity originality   importance   timeliness alignment with our mission statement

reiterate the key questions about this piece before we go over time again stop asking if this should make the cut but instead present your *why* and *how* it might make the cut   —how violent that word is when every story matters— we cut submissions   down mostly because of low funding   the heart of the argument:
inconsistent use of present tense   then an unsightly adjective   the editors want the [REDACTED INFORMATION] as if it would help   they want to ask the author where the main divide happens and suggest that we're distracted by the mis-   placed punctuation   we label it as "publishable with some technical rewrites" but even then how finished can it be with a title like   *Regret?*   the editors want to know why the dense
internal combustion   really happens right before lunch   I ask for a vote someone raises their hand   (not to vote)   to ask *was the conflict really just about video games or...*

reiterate with an owl-like precision that edits are due next month so contact the authors soon   and please cc: or bcc: me remember changes should only   be made with contributor consent   don't change their voice or style   though reiterate to the writer that changing nothing won't work   tell them their edits are due ASAP   but maybe no one will enforce this timeline (except for me)

reiterate inside my mouth the vowels I translate from Korean to English during the final push of line edits   pagination layouts   table of contents   captions   letter from the EiC   letter from the ambassador so many PDFs named the same thing I know the ins and outs of a laser printer it hums   it eats paper   it needs breaks I memorize the after-hours code to get into the office   the security guard asks when I'm planning to go home (not sure yet)   he doesn't know how much these words mean to me   and how a mistake in post-publishing ruins the issue   ruins our budget   ruins the timeline   ruins my confidence ruins   so I reread the proof one more time

reiterate the opening phrase to this poem,   three words I saved   in an email draft   a scrap of language for sometime special   it was finally time to write toward it   it's been seven years and I am finally writing toward reiteration   reiteration   this urge finally   reiterating back   to where it started   as an utter   a playfulness I wanted to hear that owl coo   I wanted to hear it again   I hear it coo it coos   then echoes   then coos again

Magpie's

My favorite bar
with its phallus-covered wall inside.

They flatter the air. I lie
every time I say I'm hungry.

A bumpy color rises in me
I go home before the taste.

All of my first dates
had to end somewhere.

Excuse me sir, I must tear
through one more glass tonight.

Bathroom break whispers:
Please don't ruin this bar.

Seals don't count. So far
I haven't licked yours shut.

You ask, *who decides what
is next?* Let's take a break.

Over so soon. Saturday tainted
by a dream of you in my womb

Our goodbye in a dark room.

I crafted my first draft
of your letter, then tore it in half.

Guro Station, Line 1

In another dream, I'm bundled up in the warmth of fish-shaped bread.
A treat in the winter. I breathe in the red bean and custard filling.
The smoke from a chestnut stand points me back toward my apartment.
I choose the subway instead. The ten-minute walk hums in my eardrum.
It always sounds like this: *Teacher, where are you going? Where is your home?*

출입문 닫겠습니다[5]

Track two sends me uptown to Gwanghwamun,
where I walk journal-in-hand past palaces
and stop to eat street food. I've had every taste
in every season. I try to hold them all in my too-small palms.

Track three drags me downtown to the sunset. After two years:
two placements, a different alphabet, hundreds of students' faces
I wonder if it is possible to love another city
or two different countries
so tightly.

이 역은 타는 곳과 전동차 사이가 넓습니다.[6]

Guro held nine roads, all leading me home. I tried to pick out
the words I knew in the poems painted on the glass doors,
feeling the breath of each train car's mouth swallowing me
and the rest of the crowd. I would do anything to go back.

내리실 때 조심합시다 바랍니다[7]

I still use the same alarm.

I wake up on time, after the subway car halts in my sleep.
I miss the way I became food on the trains entering
Guro Station, leaving crumbs in my splintering.

---

5 *Chulipmun datgetseumnida*, The doors are closing
6 *Ee yeokeun tanun gotghwa jeondongcha saeega neolseumnida*, At this station, there is a
wide gap between the platform and the train
7 *Naerishil ddae joshimhamshida baramnida*, Please be careful when exiting

I wanted to lick the
words off food
labels for days.

I wanted to be
home for good.

Upon Arrival

The morning I landed
in NYC I just wanted to curl
up and crawl into a huge black bowl
and burn. From one home to another in
14 hours. I am mixed up inside over what I
didn't say goodbye enough times to. I suggest
Korean food for lunch. I miss being so good-
mannered: tilting my bowl to have the last of
my hot soup; using two hands to pass the com-
munal kimchi dish and keeping my chopsticks
out of the hardened rice I tried not to eat. I
wish I could drink myself out of this bowl
while I'm still scalding hot so I don't feel
me on the way down. I miss my
tongue. How swollen it got
from a soup burn.

New Jersey
after Craig Morgan Teicher

At first, I thought the past was leaping out to haunt me
deep in the back pockets of my journals and sewing kits.

I heard it first. A murmuring stream growing into the Atlantic
Ocean, the shrill wind shaking billboards and powerlines.

Behind me, I felt it. The breath of October fog edging
up against my spine, undoing my hair, my repeated shivers.

Though the things I remember might not have happened,
like the evacuation, the Raritan River bridge underwater

the hydroplaning cars flooding the parkway.
Lights, and then no lights.

When I woke up, I traced your face
in the reflection of Lake Lenape.

We sat there and I scrolled through the census the year before
only 2,135 neighbors around us. You must have known

I was always bound to end up in a big city, not far from the water
and the voice I save on my answering machine actually

sounds relenting now, as if all the malice I expect
when I open that honey jar in that shoebox

you covered with lines from my favorite poems
wasn't the only thing that was left there all those years ago.

Bilateral Stimulation

> *When a traumatic event occurs, the brain can lock this memory in isolation.*
> *The original images, sounds, thoughts, beliefs, and emotions can't leave. This*
> *prevents healing from taking place. EMDR can simulate REM sleep,*
> *which helps the brain process unconscious material.*
> —*Eye Movement Desensitization Reprocessing (EMDR) Protocol*

When I sit in Stephanie's office, I try to figure out
why I can't bring myself to drive.

> I call upon my grandfather to keep me safe.
> He comes back as a grasshopper every time.

The golden hour splatters my face
as she adjusts the curtain, though my eyes remain closed.

> I'm in full gear: a buzzer in each hand, headphones
> cradling my skull, a pillow on my lap.

Stephanie adjusts the equipment notch by notch.
Vibration strength: seven. Pace: six.

> Volume: one. She reads the protocol every week,
> though I already know what to expect.

With each set of bilateral stimulation,
I go back deeper into the headlines and empty homes.

> I fly cross-country every year for my dad's birthday,
> months of dread welling up in my throat.

I search for Band-Aids and ammonia inhalant
clear drawers of half-used soap bars and lipstick.

> When we drive to Atlantic City, I avoid
> eye contact and cover my tattoos.

He asks why I still don't drive and grows angry.
I crumple into the backseat like I always have with his speed.

> What should be a milestone of freedom is locked
> inside me as an intense fear: to lose my body,

21

to lose someone else's body. Mistake after mistake,
I still got my license. I learn who I really am

                        every time I shake. I grasp at the knowing breath,
                          the headless nausea, the thoughts that come up:

I will hurt someone. I will lose control.
I will die. I accept this as truth

                                          Until it's not.

Help me.

                         I tap in my grandfather, the grasshopper:
                strong brave pulses, my palm full of lightning,

left-right-left-right. He lands on my dad's
hands gripping the steering wheel.

                   My grandfather stops the car from swerving,
                            gentles my dad's voice.

Stephanie says, *good, go with that.*
My chest opening, my stomach calling: *I'm alive.*

Re:

> Last night
> I dreamt
> of a poem
> I wrote to you
> on a plane
> a year ago

Last January in Gangnam, at Oz Board Game Cafe,
we built train lines by playing Ticket to Ride until
the owner said *you've been playing the wrong way*

> Before you
> my weekends were perfect
> successions of Americanos

You said *I had always wanted to travel*
I said *I never wanted to leave America*
You asked me *why do you work so hard*
I said *I don't know, I'm in love with being tired*

> After you
> I bought fewer groceries
> we traded poems over dinner

You wrote *of every favor, I ask but one*
don't forget me while you're gone
I wrote *though I'm miles away I'm not really gone*
you'll see me every day, in each rising sun

> Twelve months later
> I moved across America

Upon landing
I hit send

> I wonder what you're doing now

You replied
steady and smooth
I miss you.

December

after Natalie Diaz

It is December and we must be brave.

In the twinkling lights of The City by the Bay
I can see where the inlets stop the power supply.
The city's howling bridge: what the engineers call
an aerodynamic phenomenon. Golden hue majestic
enough to disguise the suicide nets below.

The tree—always fake until this year—drops its needles
and clutches the Win Long Hardware Store string lights.
I braid wicks and pour wax into yogurt containers,
sift through magazines and slice dancers away from their stage.

The things I know aren't easy:
a sibling neck-deep in conspiracy theories
a father nauseous to the touch
a mother in N95 masks every night.
I curate a found family in my adulthood.

I fly six hours and visit the house on Lavender Drive.
The neighborhood streets are full of namesakes: Wintergreen,
Azalea, Periwinkle, Honeysuckle, Ivy, Oak, Boxwood.
What was once a small crack in the sidewalk erupted with weeds.
How can I call this a home if nobody says
we need to let go of what we never had.

If we are what we love, what does love look like unreturned?
Is it me? I spread love with my tongue licking envelopes
which is why I still write letters and buy postcards from every state.

The first incandescent light bulb illuminated my hometown,
a little known fact by people who still live there.
This is why I dread going to Stop and Shop or Dunkin' Donuts
where I am no longer nameless in front of my classmate's kid.

What is happiness if not the absence of natural disasters—
a lack of power outages and reliable clean water.
I open entire drawers filled with hospital soap bars and inkless pens.
I beg my mom to throw them out. *But in Cebu, the kids will need this.*
I read about Typhoon Odette and how it chewed up then spit out their houses.

We heat our food on scratched up Corelle dishes
then transfer it to the dishes from Mikasa with gold trim.
Once, I made a plate spark like lightning in the microwave.
I feel like that sometimes: breakable, explosive.

In between spoonfuls of *sinigang*, my dad asks me again:
Why are you still afraid to drive? Meaning, *What did we do wrong?*
as if Martha's picture isn't still on my wall,
the New York Times headline fresh:
Young Dancers in Speeding Car Leave a Long Trail of Grief.

The cloudless sky beckons the streetlamp to turn on.
It hiccups until it offers a path from Lavender Drive
toward Wintergreen Avenue, winnowing through the neighborhood
to feed the mouth of the Garden State Parkway.

Somewhere far from Ilaya, Dumanjug, Cebu,
an American family cleans up the dinner table,
Saran-wrapping leftover *kare-kare* and steak.
The placemats, sticky with vinegar, read
There's No Place Like Home.

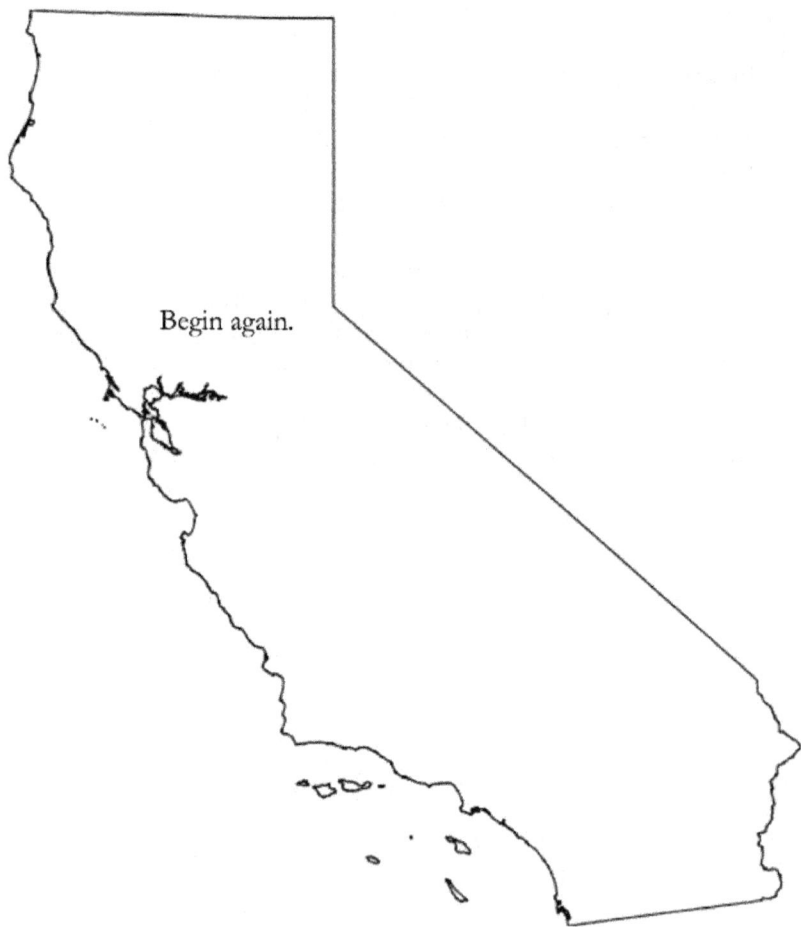

Begin again.

Muse

The ink spills thickest before it runs dry before it stops writing at all.
—Theresa Hak Kyung Cha, Dictee

I searched for you in California, my purple Jansport backpack in tow.
Back then, I wasn't so scared of strangers. I trusted anyone who knew
your name, who touched your book. I asked them what still stays with them:
a splintered country, a family's migration, muses, heroines, or martyrs?

I watched your hands gathering and ungathering dirt and sand,
the ring on your finger in and out of view. I queue up your video cassettes:
Re Dis Appearing, Mouth to Mouth, White Dust from Mongolia, Permutations.
I watched them the way you intended: dark room, multi-channel TVs.
I watched your hands light candles, your hair running down your spine.
I took notes on your voice, held your photo negatives with my gloved hands.

I think about your living body and follow it to the ends of the earth.
The first thing I did when I got to Busan, South Korea, was see a film.
You were still young when you had to leave, the middle child of five.
Before the first sunrise of that year, I wandered out onto the beach with a
balloon in hand, and wondered how close I was to your childhood home.

I visit Artists Space in New York where your memorial was, your body
found not quite fresh in the Puck Building's basement a mile away.
You never showed up to dinner, your book displayed on St. Mark's Place
where your friends were waiting and waiting. From the DNA under
your fingernails, we knew you fought back. Your ruby wedding ring gone.

I searched for you in San Francisco, met your brother at Cafe Trieste.
San Francisco was another hometown for you, my home now for six years.
After all these years I still scan bookshelves for your name, walk up
staircases thinking of you. I revisit your book when I fly around the world
only to return back to the place I came from. In another life, we'd have met.
I would have hammered nails into the museum wall for your installations.
I would have rethreaded your artist books with new burlap string.

I know you like this because even now, 31 years after your death,
I retrace your steps back into the basement where your art was born
and you come alive when I visit your archive, or stand in front of your school,
or when I tell your story to everyone who will listen.

Dear Violet

You were born in the summer

　　　　　　　　　　in a vacation town prone to fires.

I was waiting for the bus with your mother

　　　　　　　　　who was waiting for you to come back.

Your father drove off with her breast milk

　　　　　　　　　so he could feed you on the run.

She didn't know where you two went

　　　　　　　　　　maybe to the place where

　　　　　　　　　　Nevada meets California

or maybe somewhere further away.

　　　　　　　　　Your mother asked me for the time

　　　　　　　　　and if I'd like an egg roll.

I decline

　　　　　　　　　and check the bus schedule again.

Your mother apologized for the question

said she wasn't offering this to me

"because you're Asian."

　　　　　　　　　She complimented the sweet, old

　　　　　　　　　Panda Express cashier's bracelet

　　　　　　　　　and received extra food in return.

My mom uses food to communicate with me.

                    Your mom wanted to communicate with me.

I think anything is forgivable

when it finally rains in Lake Tahoe.

                    After 30 minutes, we're still waiting

                    and I learn more about you.

You've been missing for two days

the apartment so full of your scent

lingering on diapers made of t-shirts.

                    Your mother turns down my embrace

                    just in case you make it home soon.

We board the bus and Joel, our driver,

encourages her not to drink too much.

                    She was almost one year sober

                    until today.

We ride the bus around Donner Lake

and your mother asks if any bodies

have turned up lately

                    as if you might be one.

I see Joel's face in the rear-view mirror

fishing for the right thing to say.

He wants to know your name.

Your mother's favorite color was purple

and so you became Violet.

Queen of Scars

I used to hold negatives up to the light, smearing my face with my
with my fingertips, discovering how gelatin undoes these scenes

after twenty years. Now my thumb and pointer finger kiss
then stretch my face beyond recognition, pixeling out

the deep pits of acne blemishes,
the moon crater above my lip.

After all my skin has been through,
I still believe I can own my own life.

I wasn't always complicit in the cuts on my legs
wrist or neckline, the routes crisscrossing my hips.

I rubbed in Sebo de Macho to make them fade,
to make sure one day they would stop being displayed.

I worked my wounds in circles to conjure up
the magic of hypertrophic healing.

I rubbed myself raw like a cherry splitting between teeth.
My girlhood was precious, risking the warmth before the burn.

I collected the heartbeats of near-death slices
and the moisture of before-life breaths.

When it gets too quiet, I go looking for my scars
digging for them, like a fever lying in wait.

Dawn Angelicca Barcelona is a Filipina-American writer from New Jersey. She is a winner of the San Francisco Foundation/Nomadic Press Literary Award (2022) and *Epiphany's* Fresh Voices Fellowship (2023). She's currently a candidate in the Litowitz MFA+MA Program at Northwestern University. Her work can be read in *Atlanta Review, Red Ogre Review, Epiphany, 2River View, SUSPECT,* and *Brink.* She is an alumna of the Sewanee Writers' Conference, Juniper Summer Writers' Institute, Fulbright Program to South Korea, Community of Writers at Olympic Valley, VONA, Kenyon Review Writers Workshop, and Kearny Street Workshop's Interdisciplinary Writers Lab. dawnangelicca.com